Soccer or Basketball

Dona Herweck Rice

Publishing Credits

Rachelle Cracchiolo, M.S.Ed., *Publisher*
Conni Medina, M.A.Ed., *Managing Editor*
Nika Fabienke, Ed.D., *Content Director*
Véronique Bos, *Creative Director*
Shaun N. Bernadou, *Art Director*
Carol Huey-Gatewood, M.A.Ed., *Editor*
John Leach, *Assistant Editor*
Courtney Roberson, *Senior Graphic Designer*

Image Credits: All images from iStock and/or Shutterstock.

Teacher Created Materials
5301 Oceanus Drive
Huntington Beach, CA 92649-1030
www.tcmpub.com
ISBN 978-1-4938-9863-3
© 2019 Teacher Created Materials, Inc.

Which of these is

your ,  ?

ball   soccer
         player

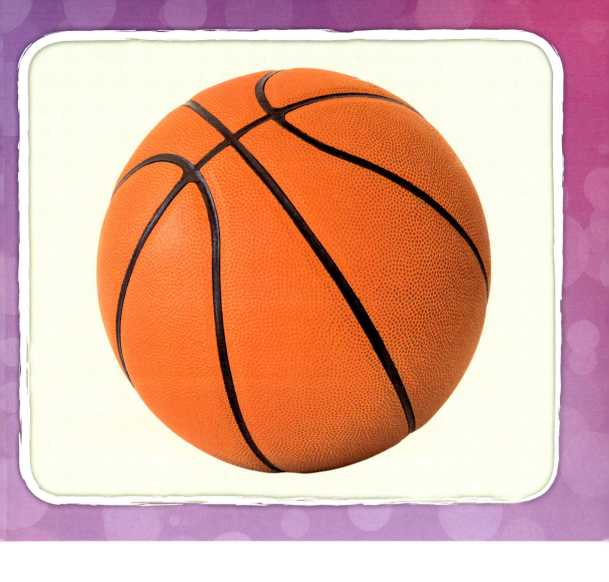

Which of these is your  , ?

shoe　　basketball player

Which of these is

your , ?

net   basketball player

Which of these is your ,  ?

team   soccer player

Which of these is your , ?

trophy   basketball player

High-Frequency Words

New Words

these
which
your

Review Words

is
of